Alicia Rodriguez

TABLE OF CONTENTS

A Pelican Book

Teaching Tips for Caregivers and Teachers:

Research shows that one of the best ways for students to learn a new topic is to read about it.

Before Reading

- Read the title and predict what the book will be about.
- Read the "Words to Know" and discuss the meaning of each word.
- Read the back cover to see what the book is about.

During Reading

- When a student gets to a word that is unknown, ask them to look at the rest of the sentence to find clues to help with the meaning of the unknown word.
- Motivate students with praise and encouragement.

After Reading

- Discuss the main idea of the book.
- Ask students to give one detail that they learned in the book.

Sight Words

a
all
and
are
big
black
blue
brown
eat
far
fly
green
have
is
lay
like
long
most
or
small
some
they
this
to
too
white

Words to Know

eggs

peacock

plants

purple

tail feathers

This is a **peacock**.

peacock

Some peacocks are blue, green, black, or **purple**.

purple

They have long **tail feathers**.

tail feathers

Some peacocks have small brown and white tail feathers.

All peacocks like to eat **plants**.

plants

Some peacocks lay **eggs**.

Most peacocks are too big to fly far!

Index

Written by: Alicia Rodriguez
Design by: Under the Oaks Media
Series Development: James Earley
Editor: Kim Thompson

Photos: Shutterstock: Sunti: cover; LittleDogKorat: p. 5; jctabb: p. 7; pr2is: p. 9; Virendra30: p. 11; Sean Sebastian: p. 13; veranji: p. 14; Karornyot Wildlife Photography

Library of Congress PCN Data
Peacocks / Alicia Rodriguez
Asian Animals
ISBN 978-1-63897-437-6(hard cover)
ISBN 978-1-63897-552-6(paperback)
ISBN 978-1-63897-667-7(EPUB)
ISBN 978-1-63897-782-7(eBook)
Library of Congress Control Number: 2022933687

Printed in the United States of America.

Seahorse Publishing Company
www.seahorsepub.com

Published in the United States
Seahorse Publishing
PO Box 771325
Coral Springs, FL 33077